All That Once Was You

poems by

Thomas Griffin

Finishing Line Press
Georgetown, Kentucky

All That Once Was You

Copyright © 2018 by Thomas Griffin
ISBN 978-1-63534-582-7 First Edition
All rights reserved under International and Pan-American Copyright Conventions.
No part of this book may be reproduced in any manner whatsoever without written permission from the publisher, except in the case of brief quotations embodied in critical articles and reviews.

ACKNOWLEDGMENTS

Grateful Acknowledgment is made to the editors of the following publications in which these poems first appeared, sometimes in somewhat different form, and for their generous support of this work and of contemporary poetry in general.

About Place Journal: Tree Sense

Letters to the River: The Praises Of This Place

Lotus.zine: Lovelife

Penumbra: A Question, When The Demons Come Out

Summation 2016/17: Arriving

the Aurorean: The Passing (Pushcart Nominee)

Though the author of a collection of poetry does most of the heavy lifting this one easily rests upon the shoulders of many supporters. Deep gratitude to the following who were recipients of early drafts and allies of these final versions: Bill Pelz-Walsh, Sparrow Hart, Renee Adams, Robert O'Sullivan Schleith, Jeanne Marie Walsh, Jerry Levy, Alan Steinberg, Jonathan Klein, Ann Buckingham, Kate Gleason, et al. And to Cynthia Brackett-Vincent, editor of *the Aurorean* for the Pushcart nomination.

For my children, Ana and Kai, and grandchildren, Thisbe and Eva.

Publisher: Leah Maines
Editor: Christen Kincaid
Cover Art: Thomas Griffin
Author Photo: Joanna Moyer-Battick
Cover Design: Elizabeth Maines McCleavy

Printed in the USA on acid-free paper.
Order online: www.finishinglinepress.com
　　　　　also available on amazon.com

Author inquiries and mail orders:
Finishing Line Press
P. O. Box 1626
Georgetown, Kentucky 40324
U. S. A.

Table of Contents

Winging Thru Darkness 1

If Not You 2

When The Demons Come Out 3

Everything You Hold Onto 4

The Night Mists Of Summer 5

Be Still In This Loneliness 6

Trying Not To Step In 7

The Passing 8

A Question 9

Unexpected Gift 10

Hangbird 11

Everyone Is Waiting In The Field 12

Arriving 13

Lovers At First Sight 14

Hands 15

Direction 16

The Poetry in Living 17

The Praises of this Place 18

From August to the Moon 19

Tree Sense 20

River Gift 21

Picture This 22

The Embrace Of Love 23

True Friend 24

Lovelife 25

*In loving memory of my gifted mentor and dear friend,
Donald Sheehan.*

Winging Thru Darkness

You say you know
that every beginning starts
with an open palm.

Then, have you the faith
to reach for that door
the simple commitment
of raising a hand
on your behalf?

How? Tell me how
you will find the latch
winging thru this darkness
with such hesitant hands?
With what effort
will its lock tumble free?

When the time to act comes
don't be the foolish past
take heart, drop every dark memory
you hold onto.

If Not You

A black-handed crow
winging through fine rain—
taking a trip you fear

raindrops wailing upon the windshield
the broken mouths of dry brown grasses
every tree's leaves knuckled down—

bring your boat upon the shore

the quince is heavy with bloody blossom—

keep looking, stay awake
gather by the gate with the cows

thirsty corn rows stiffen along the roadside—
hope the journey home is shorter

and suddenly the shiny black road is empty—

look, stare for hours

the puckered lake relaxes
back into itself, smooth
no longer troubled—

who will be here
if not you?

When The Demons Come Out

You say your life is wonderful
perfect in every way: you're a
pearl pendant hanging from life's lobe.
You have no idea what life is all about.

Wait till your cupboards are out of cash
and your trash bin is empty of offal—
you don't know what arms are for
until life sticks the needle of need in your veins
and you can't find a dealer.

Remember when your mother called you a slut
and kicked you out? Or lying in your crib
listening to that horrible echo
it's good for the baby to cry,
teaches him what life is all about.

Oh, yes! The demons are out now
aren't they? And they remember everything.

Everything You Hold Onto

These desolate streets running
back and forth through that hole

in your chest, these blacked-out
houses with their blank tables, their

empty chairs and along the driveways
snow banks piled higher than hope:

this city is your life, just this moment
of your life. Leave your car in the garage

don't be afraid, don't run, don't worry that
the sun won't come again, it's only

this short season of life's indifference.
Can you embrace its chill? You will die from

everything you hold onto. Nothing
is held long in an infant's hand.

The Night Mists Of Summer

In a short while
you will fall asleep

the river of desire
will not be found
except in a dream

where a stone wall runs
between the black
legs of trees, away
into the dark.

A gray mist seeps
across a field of fireflies
snaps the lightning in two, as
a sudden heavy rain floods the gutters.

To die now seems endurable
for what have you become?
A job, a father, a mother, a solution?

Be Still In This Loneliness

Look at you, knocking at the door of *no one home* again
whether anyone answers makes no difference
yet you keep on rapping that innocent tapping.

Drive away, fast, I beg you
this shard of shame will speed its way to your heart
keep knocking and die.

Worry about this lost love later on
that dog will bark as soon as you make your presence known
so flee, dear heart, find somewhere to be still in this loneliness.

Trying Not To Step In

There isn't a bridge across
the wide world could span
the two lives you're living.
Depression? An invitation
to swim in the shifting water
you're trying not to step in.
The center of your life
doesn't give a damn
what you want to look like—
its sole purpose is to look like itself.
See that moon hand, that bright palm
floating across the dark ocean?
Take it, let it drag you under.
Down there with crustacean dreams
that's where you belong now.

The Passing

A chilling wind pulls the dark hands of the pond up into the sky
the beaver lolls in the black, comfortable depths
as a great blue heron flaps past the farther shore
rising slowly, gliding to its gray nest of driftwood
among the dead trees. Only a few cattails left
their furry seeds still clinging to the brittle shaft.
If I could I would take you down
to the silence, the quietly breathing bottom
and the dark green shoots the mallard plucks
as he tips his white rump skyward and plunges
beak and eyes among the idly swaying grasses of that deep quiet.
Your clothes will not protect you from the first shock
as you dive to the calling darkness and that first moment of living
and looking back the wind has sealed the place where you entered
with its hush and the rushing of waves behind you
and the passing of all that once was you.

A Question

Which seed are you?

The one that even fire
can't destroy? Or

are you the seed
that rots first

missed in moist ground
till a bold shoot bolts

into sunlight?
Do you drift without care

across strange fields
falling through darkness

like stars?
Are you the one who

knows the husk
and not the center

who forgets to be a tree
and lives in the dark

dreaming of green wings
flying through the night air

or are you the seed
that knows nothing

but to abandon dreams of then
for the cocky shaft of now?

Unexpected Gift

You take the path down to the river
where the cold morning air
is charged with the sound of rushing
and the smell of ice melting.

The dry hard ground
slaps your senses.
Now you know the fear of the old
dying alone in their beds.
You go down to the river

because there is no place else to go.
No other arms will hold you
no other ears heed this sorrow
no other lover fortify
your faltering heart.

All without question.
To have a love such as this
and a path that takes you there often—
this unexpected gift of living.

Hangbird

Listen,
the center of your life is fire
feel your flaming heart
pulsing beneath your present thoughts

and make way for *change*.
Let it build a springtime nest
all broken strings and matted dreams
dangling high up in this hidden place inside you
safe from the whispers of doubt.

Everyone Is Waiting In The Field

Always someone—
a letter, a hand wave
someone sweeping the floor.

People are kind
then you notice.

Dismiss the thief who
guards your timorous heart—
everyone is waiting in the field.

The moon refuses
downcast looks

sings those songs for which
you are weeping.

Arriving

We will not speak of such things as the soul
        leaving the body, nor the
thousand ideas unheard
        nor the tocsin of a sister
too soon deceased

        no, we will not share speech
things found in a pocket, nor the
        shadow the sea erases from shore.
What blinds us may someday
        come into focus

all we can say for certain
        is that arriving takes a long time.

Lovers At First Sight

Any day now, that rain
that penciled message
scribbled and forgotten
on the calendar
will arrive in a sudden
rending of the black sky
and all at once
you and your life will meet
like lover's at first sight
oh! you can be certain of that.

Hands

Look at your hands
these long tan strands of sand
falling through your fingers;
how often
you have tried to make solid
these shifting plans for your life;
the tighter your grasp
the more directions your life leaks out
on its crazy wildly careening course.

Direction

The hour is late
all the worries of the day
tucked in their bed asleep
you come to rest at last under lamplight.

Year after year you have tried
to live a life of this moment
but instead have been tricked
by this goalless game of trying.

Now you understand that a moment lives us.
Everything hoped for, every grand scheme
a pebble in the shoe of living
a memory passed over.

Wonder no more. No need
to inspect the workmanship
rest, now, in
the fullness of this.

The Poetry in Living

Those intoxicated moths
flitting white wings circling
the summer streetlight—
you could be them—
there is poetry inside you.

Without poetry, you merely exist
sleeping under the freeway
in a cardboard box beside your roaring
refusal to stop and hear what is wrong
with your life.

One day soon you will
cease this drunken binge
worrying over things
every other animal ignores.
Your lovely heart silenced
no longer trebling to the indictments
of priests and presidents—

at last you sense the only truth—
poetry was yours every moment
but you kept looking for silverware
and starved your whole life.
No! There was never a time
that poetry was not
down under the freeway
beside your cardboard life
calling, *Come to me
and I will make you whole.*

The Praises of this Place

If not now
when? Who will sing
the praises of this place
if not you?
Can you make love
with limp excuses?
Just one word
in your own voice
would cock the heads of robins
but today
they listen only to worms.
Every morning a thousand birds
give the world a chorus of themselves
without hesitation or regret
all through the day
the trees and sky
speak in the hushed voices of lovers
and in the night
the grasses sigh in the warm hands
of the evening breeze
while fireflies flash their honest love
to the distant stars passing overhead—
when you are ready
come join the conversation.

From August to the Moon

Give yourself to this perfection:
only the sky as it pulls night
over your sleepy head
knows constancy, can teach
a lover's eyes
to envision stars, a moon
even a black moon.

Where will you root
in these granite hills?
Skinned with destiny
knowing only this thirst
this hunger for the rhapsody of being.
Look at your wrist
a compound of multiples
fragments of motion
seeming firm if wrists weren't
to beg breaking.

The solid thing is
that nothing is solid.
The valley, the mountain
bother with none.
Cheerful in Autumn
the clouds grow more themselves
and fill their pockets with snow.

Tree Sense

See how it makes
itself
a huge and glorious
thing
light and rain
earth and animal;
that tree
made from what is
around it
beautiful
not because
it stands alone
but as a forest
of things that belong
to each other.

River Gift

Led by a longing for searing sun
    the catcalls of gulls above laughing water
       you push off from shore and
join the river stealing to the sea. Unmoored
       bobbing along this mysterious current
    who knows the course of your wondrous heart?
Today, you wander unanchored by weighty questions
        drifting without worry downstream.

Picture This

Please, don't tell me you don't understand.
I know you:
one way in and one way out.
I can explain both.

Be patient.
You will begin over and over again:
start to know something and forget
start to know something and...

It's only
fear dashing through your dark veins
telling you what you don't want to hear.

What can I say?
You're just human?
Breathe?

Picture this:
a windowpane with no glass
a field full of brown stubble
blue swathed hills and a glaze
of silver above those trees

you float above it all
forgiven. No one you have failed
remembers.

It's only love, it's only
all the things you can't name
that...
that...
you don't know, yet.

The Embrace Of Love

How much money do you have?
It's not enough.
The price of love is high.
The thorns of this rose
you cannot buy clothes for,
nothing will stop their sting.
This love means to strip you, but
listen closely
love is a door your mother found
and opened so that you might come.

True Friend

I swear to you this one truth:
no son-of-the-one-god guides your fate
no stabbed palm asking for unfailing fealty—
get off your knees
rest in the strong sinew
search out the solid depth of bone
world-wise blood inside you—
there are no *original* stains on your soul.

The truest, sweetest love—
this life inside you
is a power that calls your name
thru every hungry pore of your body
take comfort in the steady beating
of your heart, there is no other
god but this moment of living.
Hush and hear its soothing
love for you.

Lovelife

There is no one who loves the way you do
no other child grew into this life but you
and no woman, no man, no one soul
has that destiny that you sense
that mystery rising up into
the proud flower of your body
but like an angel trying to make better wings
your life is invisible to you
while so much effort is wasted in looking.
But wonder with me, now
if you fell in love with
if you trusted in your own life
took a petal of it from deep inside
the bloom of you
would we fall silent in awe
of the precious, delicious scent of you?
This thing we speak of, this love
some will ask *how will I know it?*
some will point to how often you've failed to show it.
Still others will thump your chest
laugh at the hollow ring of worn out defenses
between your ribs—
they will call you a liar.
Don't be measured by their doubts and fears
for every one of us will come up shorter than ideal.
Listen to this one truth again and again
and drop these abstractions, these props
of the drama between you and another:
your life is to love and be loved
so wonder with me
now will you begin?

Thomas Griffin was born on a USAF base in England. His father was a MSgt, his mother was a personnel manager in state service. Beginning on Air Force bases, he's lived and worked all over the United States.

Thomas' professional life includes working as a carpenter, electrician, plumber, estate gardener, stone mason, surveyor, forester, potter and furniture maker. As a visiting artist, he has taught playwriting and performance in college, adult ed, high school and middle school programs.

As a young poet, Thomas was the first docent at The Frost Place in Franconia, NH, leading summer tours at Robert Frosts' New England home and attending poetry workshops there with Robert Hass, Gary Miranda, Richard Eberhart, William Mathews, Cleopatra Mathis, James Merrill, et al.

A keen language student, Thomas met a mentor in Classics Professor Donald Sheehan with whom he studied Greek—reading Heraclitus and Homer and Italian—reading Dante and Petrarch. While an undergrad, Thomas studied Chinese and ASL. He received a BA with honors in Language, Literature & Writing from Marlboro College and an MFA for playwriting from Goddard College.

For over 25 years, Thomas has worked professionally as a stage and film actor and for the past 17 years has been the founder and artistic director of Acting On Impulse Theatre Company; directing, lighting, set designing and producing work for regional stage. Several of his plays have been produced nationally in festivals and regional theatres.

www.ingramcontent.com/pod-product-compliance
Lightning Source LLC
LaVergne TN
LVHW041515070426
835507LV00012B/1580